GROWING UP

My First Sleepover

Charlotte Guillain

Heinemann Library
Chicago, Illinois

H www.heinemannraintree.com
Visit our website to find out
more information about
Heinemann-Raintree books.

To order:
☎ Phone 888-454-2279
🖳 Visit www.heinemannraintree.com
to browse our catalog and order online.

Edited by Dan Nunn, Rebecca Rissman, and Sian Smith
Designed by Joanna Hinton-Malivoire
Picture research by Elizabeth Alexander
Originated by Capstone Global Library Ltd
Printed and bound in the United States of America,
North Mankato, MN

15 14 13 12 11
10 9 8 7 6 5 4 3 2 1

Library of Congress Cataloging-in-Publication Data
Guillain, Charlotte.
  My first sleepover / Charlotte Guillain.
    p. cm. — (Growing up)
  Includes bibliographical references and index.
  ISBN 978-1-4329-4802-3 (hc) — ISBN 978-1-4329-4812-2
(pb) 1. Sleepovers. I. Title.
  GV1205.G85 2011
  793.2'1—dc22   2010024196

112011
006430RP

Acknowledgments
We would like to thank the following for permission
to reproduce photographs: Alamy pp. 12 (© Image
Source), 14, 23 glossary homesick (© Catchlight Visual
Services); © Capstone Publishers Ltd pp. 5, 7, 11, 19, 23
glossary host (Karon Dubke); Corbis pp. 4, 23 glossary
relative (© JLP/Jose L. Pelaez), 9 (© Tony Metaxas/
Asia Images), 15 (© Christina Kennedy/fstop), 16 (©
Nicole Hill/Rubberball); Getty Images pp. 6 (Digital
Vision), 10 (Jupiterimages/FoodPix), 13 (Jupiterimages/
Brand X Pictures); Photolibrary pp. 8 (Corbis), 17 (SW
Productions/Brand X Pictures), 18 (Juice Images);
Shutterstock pp. 20 (© Vasiliy Koval), 21, 23 glossary
operation (© Monkey Business Images).

Front cover photograph of girls at a sleepover
reproduced with permission of Alamy (© Image
Source). Back cover photographs of a bathroom
reproduced with permission of © Capstone Publishers
(Karon Dubke), and camping reproduced with
permission of Shutterstock (© Vasiliy Koval).

Every effort has been made to contact copyright
holders of material reproduced in this book. Any
omissions will be rectified in subsequent printings if
notice is given to the publisher.

Contents

Some words are shown in bold, **like this**.
You can find them in the glossary on page 23.

What Is a Sleepover?

A sleepover is when you stay overnight at someone else's house.

It could be at a friend's house or with **relatives**.

You may sleep at another house for one night, or sometimes for longer.

You may eat your dinner and breakfast at a sleepover.

Why Do People Have Sleepovers?

Many people have sleepovers for fun.

Some people have a sleepover with friends to celebrate their birthdays.

You may go to a sleepover with friends or family if your parents are away.

Your parents might have to go to the hospital or away for work or a trip.

What Do I Need to Take?

You need to take pajamas, a toothbrush, and a change of clothes.

Sometimes you might also take your own sleeping bag to sleep in.

You might take something to remind you
of home, such as a teddy bear or book.

You might like to take a photo of your
family with you.

What Do I Need to Know?

It is a good idea to know what to expect on a sleepover.

Ask your **relative** or your friend's parents what will happen during your stay.

Find out where everything is, and always ask if you need anything.

Make sure you know where the bathrooms are.

What Might Be Different?

When you sleep over somewhere else, lots of things might be different.

You might try new or unusual foods or eat meals at different times.

If you are staying with friends, it might be exciting to stay up later than normal.

You might sleep on the floor or share a room for the first time.

What Should I Do If I Miss Home?

You might miss your family and your own bedroom at home.

Tell your **relative** or friend and his or her parents if you feel **homesick**.

You might be able to call your parents on the phone to make you feel better.

Try to keep busy and have fun doing something new.

What Makes Sleepovers Fun?

Sleepovers are fun because you do things differently than you normally do.

You might eat special food together.

It is fun to see your friends in a different situation, or to spend time with a **relative**.

You might play games or watch a movie together.

What Happens at the End?

You might feel tired in the morning if you stayed up late.

You will usually have breakfast before you go home.

Make sure you remember to take all your things and say thank you to your **host**.

You might like to give the host a gift or a card to say thank you.

When Else Might I Stay Away from Home?

You might have to sleep away from home at other times.

You might go away on a school trip or go camping.

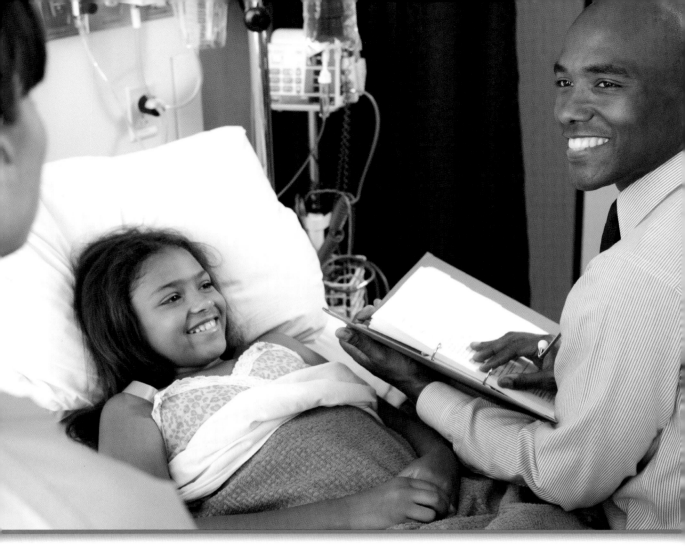

If you are sick or need an **operation**, you may have to stay in the hospital for a while.

If you have been on a sleepover, you won't feel so nervous if this happens.

What to Pack for a Sleepover

- ✓ pajamas
- ✓ change of clothes
- ✓ toothbrush
- ✓ hair brush
- ✓ towel
- ✓ sleeping bag
- ✓ teddy bear or stuffed toy
- ✓ gift for **host**

Picture Glossary

 **homesick** when someone misses his or her home and family

 **host** someone you go to stay with or visit who takes care of you and makes sure that you have the things you need

 **operation** special treatment in the hospital

 **relative** person in your family

Find Out More

Books

McGillian, Jamie Kyle. *Sleepover Party!: Games and Giggles for a Fun Night.* New York: Sterling, 2007.

Websites

You can sleepover with the dinosaurs at the American Museum of Natural History in New York:
www.amnh.org/kids/sleepovers/

Or stay at the Museum of Nature and Science in Dallas:
www.natureandscience.org/kids/sleepovers.asp

Your parents can help you find out about a sleepover in a museum near you.

Index